# 50

## fantastic things to do with
# 4-5 year olds

SALLY AND PHILL FEATHERSTONE

# Contents

Published 2010 by A&C Black Publishers Limited
36 Soho Square, London, W1D 3QY
www.acblack.com

ISBN 978-1-4081-2329-4
Copyright © A&C Black Publishers Ltd 2010

Written by Sally Featherstone and Phill Featherstone
Design by and Sally Boothroyd
Photographs © Shutterstock with the exception of:
Pg 41 © sdenness/Fotolia; Pg 52 © Vadim
Ponomarenko/Fotolia; Pg 63 © alexandre zveiger/
Fotolia; Pg 74 © Stephanie Frey/Fotolia

Printed in Great Britain by Latimer Trend &
Company Limited

A CIP record for this publication is available from the
British Library.

The right of the authors to be identified as the
authors of this work has been asserted in accordance
with Sections 77 and 78 of the Copyright, Designs and
Patents Act, 1988.

This book is produced using paper that is made from wood grown inmanaged, sustainable forests. It is natural, renewable and recyclable. The logging and manufacturing processes conform to the environmental regulations of the country of origin.

To see our full range of titles
Visit www.acblack.com/featherstone

# Introduction

There's plenty of research to show that babies and children who enjoy a stimulating home environment learn better and more quickly. So what parents and carers do to lay the groundwork for learning early on is an investment that pays back throughout their child's life.

This book has been specially written for parents to use with their young children at home. However, it can also be used by carers and workers in nurseries and childcare settings. It contains 50 simple activities that can be done easily with very little equipment, often in odd moments of time. It's not a course to work through. All the ideas here are suitable for children from 40-60 months, and in many cases beyond.

Choose what you and your child enjoy as one of the main aims of this book is fun! There are few things as delightful or rewarding as being alongside young children as they explore, enquire, experiment and learn. Join them in their enthusiasm for learning!

There are four books in the 50 Fantastic Things series:

**50 Fantastic Things to Do With Babies** (suitable for use from soon after birth to 20 months)

**50 Fantastic Things to Do With Toddlers** (suitable for use from 16–36 months)

**50 Fantastic Things to Do With Pre-Schoolers** (suitable for use from 36–50 months)

**50 Fantastic Things to Do With Four and Five Year Olds** (suitable for use from 40–60+ months)

The age groupings above are approximate and are only suggestions. Children develop at different speeds. They also grow in spurts, with some periods of rapid development alternating with other times when they don't seem to change as quickly. So don't worry if your baby doesn't seem ready for a particular activity. Try another instead and return to it later. On the other hand, if your baby gets on well and quickly, try some of the ideas in the 'Another idea' and 'Ready for more?' sections.

# A NOTE ON SAFETY

Care must be taken at all times when dealing with young children. Common sense will be your main guide, but here are a few ideas to help you have fun safely.

Although rare, swallowing objects or choking on them are hazards. Some children are more susceptible than others.

Young children's lungs are delicate. They need clean air. *Never* smoke near your child, and don't allow anyone else to do so.

Children are naturally inquisitive and you will want to encourage this. However, secure and happy children are often unaware of danger. Your child needs you to watch out for them. Make sure you are always there. You can't watch your child all the time, but don't leave him/her alone and unsupervised for more than a few minutes at a time. Even when they are asleep check on them regularly.

The objects and toys we suggest here have been chosen for their safety. Nevertheless, most things can be dangerous if they go wrong or are not used properly. Please take care.

# Catch and kick
## simple ball play

**What is your child learning?**

### What you need:

- a ball or a beanbag – you can make a simple beanbag by filling an old sock with uncooked rice, tying it securely with an elastic band or string, and cutting off any excess sock

### WHAT TO DO:

*This game needs little preparation and a small space. It's very good for children who are getting fidgety and restless, and can be as energetic as you wish!*

1. Take your ball or beanbag and gently start a game with your child, rolling it to them and waiting for them to roll it back to you.

2. If you have space, start to gently throw the ball to each other.

3. Now you can invent some more moves, such as standing up and rolling the ball between your legs.

**Another idea:** Take this activity out of doors. Take a beanbag or ball with you to the park, the beach, even on holiday. It doesn't take up much room and will be great for a quick game (even if your flight is delayed or it is raining outside your caravan!).

*Taking turns in simple games is a vital skill for life. Your child needs to learn this, and simple practice in throwing and catching will really help. Encourage them to watch the ball all the time and use both hands. Once your child can catch reliably with two hands, try one-handed catches.*

### Ready for more?

Find a bucket or a cardboard box and make up some more games such as rolling or throwing the ball into the container.

Play with toy cars, rolling them back and forth or into a box, or use a beachball to play roll and stop.

### HELPFUL HINTS

Some children find rolling and catching difficult, if your child does, play with two adults, or an older child. One player sits behind the child and helps with catching.

'Koosh' balls (with rubber 'strings' all over them) are soft and easy to catch. If your child has poor grip, try one of these.

DID YOU
KNOW?
*Catching with both hands comes before catching with one hand.*

# Thread it through
## threading practice

### *What you need:*

- *string, wool or shoe laces*
- *objects with holes, such as:*
  - *dry macaroni or other pasta with holes*
  - *beads*
  - *washers*
  - *crisps or cereal with holes*
- *bowls to keep the objects in one place*

### WHAT TO DO:

1. Tie a big knot or a bead at the end of the string. Make sure this is big enough to stop the other objects falling off! Shoelaces are easy to use, as they have stiffened ends. If you are using wool or string, wind some sticky tape round the end to make it stiffer and easier for threading.

2. Show your child the objects you have collected for threading.

3. Now let them experiment with making a string or necklace of objects.

4. Talk about what they are doing as they work, and make a necklace yourself.

**Another idea:** Look in charity shops for strings of big beads (wash them in the dishwasher before using them).

### Ready for more?

If you make food strings, hang these in the garden for the birds.

### HELPFUL HINTS

Try big wooden beads or cotton reels, which are easier to thread. Get cheap packs of thread from bargain shops.

Help your child if they need it, by holding their hands and guiding the string through the holes. Use plenty of praise, and wear the necklace with pride!

What is your child learning?

*Using both hands is an important skill, particularly for writing, and needs lots of practice. Watch carefully and give plenty of praise for concentration and perseverance, but stop when they have had enough, or you will risk frustration.*

DID YOU
**KNOW?**
*Using both hands stimulates both sides of the brain, making it work harder.*

# Playing pairs
## a simple game to make and play

### *What you need:*

- *some magazines, catalogues or junk mail*
- *scissors*
- *card from cereal packets*
- *a glue stick*

### Ready for more?

Add some more cards to make the game more challenging.

Do the same activity with a set of photo cards of familiar objects from your home and family.

### What is your child learning?

*Playing games involves your child in learning to concentrate and remember. You are an important model to them, both as a game player and as a partner, enjoying games together.*

### WHAT TO DO:

1. Cut some card into squares of about 7cm$^2$.

2. Sit with your child and look for some matching pictures in the magazines. Make sure they can match the pictures you find. Choose simple pictures such as two dogs or two biscuits.

3. Cut the pictures out, and help your child to stick each picture on a square of card. Start with about six pairs.

4. Clear your table or a space on the floor, and spread the cards out so you can have a good look at them.

5. Now mix up the cards and spread them *face down*.

### DID YOU KNOW?

*Looking for similarities and differences is a key skill for reading.*

6. Take turns to turn over two cards. If they match, keep them, if not, turn them back.

7. The player with the most cards wins.

**Another idea:** Cut game cards from food packages.

### HELPFUL HINTS

You may need to start with a smaller number of cards, perhaps just two pairs, to give your child time to get used to the game.

Winning is great, but being a good loser is an important lesson to learn. Make sure they get a chance to win, but not always!

# You're my favourite!
## a personal photo book

### What is your child learning?

*Learning about yourself is a very important part of growing up for your child.*

### *What you need:*

- *a camera and printer*

*and EITHER*

- *a small slip-page photo album and a pen, computer labels or white paper*

*OR*

- *a plain notebook, a glue stick and a felt pen*

### WHAT TO DO:

1. Talk with your child about making a photo book of their favourite things.

2. Collect all their favourite things together in one place – favourite food, books, toys, clothes, bedtime toys etc. Let them choose and try not to influence them.

3. When you have all the things together, take a photo of each one. Your child could take the photos of they want to.

4. When you have taken photos of all the objects, take a photo of your child for the front of the book

5. Print the photos, and let your child stick or slip the photos in the album in the order they want.

6. Ask them what they want to write by each picture and either use sticky labels or write on the pages. Let them do the writing if they want to.

7. Stick their photo on the front, with their name and age or the date.

**Another idea:** Make one of these books each year as your child grows up. They will make great mementos of childhood which your child will look at again and again.

### Ready for more?

Make the photos into a computer album. You could use Word or Powerpoint, so you can put words with the photos.

### HELPFUL HINTS

Some children find it really difficult to choose, so you may need to gently prompt them.

### DID YOU KNOW?

Looking at this book over and over again will make memories stronger.

# I like it!
## making choices

**DID YOU KNOW?**
Making choices is a key skill and will help your child practise decision making.

### What you need:

- a variety of snack foods, such as apple slices, carrot sticks, little biscuits, grapes, raisins, small breads
- bowls or plates for each food
- plastic beakers
- two different drinks – such as water and juice or water and milk
- small jugs or bottles for the drinks

### WHAT TO DO:

1. Collect all the snack items and put them on a table or other surface where your child can see them.

2. Now invite your child to choose their own snack. Encourage them to say what they would like before helping themselves to one of the foods and pouring themselves one of the drinks.

3. Praise them for thinking and choosing.

4. Join in the snack yourself, saying what you are going to choose before taking it.

5. Now ask them if they would like some more snacks and follow the same process, naming before taking food and drinks.

6. Praise good table manners such as not talking with their mouth full.

**Another idea:** Put the different foods in a divided tray, such as an egg box or other plastic container with sections.

### Ready for more?

Make some yogurt dip and offer different sorts of vegetable sticks and breadsticks to dip in it.

Increase the choices and offer your child the choice of 'two at a time' snacks.

### HELPFUL HINTS

Limit the choice to two items, and offer the food before you offer the choice of drinks. Some children find it really difficult to choose, even from two alternatives.

If your child really can't choose, let them decide which they will have 'first'!

### What is your child learning?

*When your child goes to nursery or school, they will be offered choices for at least part of the day. Give them plenty of praise for decisions about all sorts of things at home.*

# It's for you!
## telephone play

**What you need:**

- *two toy phones, or old mobiles with the batteries removed.*

**Ready for more?**

Ask some more complex 'open' questions – those that need more than a 'yes or no' answer.

**WHAT TO DO:**

1. This game is good to play in a quiet place, so turn off the TV or radio when you play, so your child is not distracted.

2. Take a telephone each and sit where you can see each other's faces.

3. Start the game by saying 'Ring, ring. Hello, are you there?'

4. Your child will almost certainly join in this game with enthusiasm.

5. When they answer their phone, ask them a simple question.

6. Continue the conversation as long as they are interested. Make it fun, say some silly things as well as asking questions.

7. Remember to say goodbye to each other at the end of the call.

**Another idea:** Sit a favourite soft toy or teddy on your knee and pretend the call is from them, using a suitable 'pretend' voice and asking some relevant questions.

What is your child learning?

*Being able to take turns in conversations will help your child throughout their life, not just at home, in nursery and at school. Praise them for waiting for their turn in conversations and not 'butting in'. Giving a relevant answer to a simple question is also a skill!*

## HELPFUL HINTS

If your child does not understand the rules of the game, sit nearer and go slowly, helping them to take turns in the conversation.

Taking turns in conversations is a difficult skill for some children to learn. Go slowly and give them plenty of practice.

# Coloured ribbons
## movements with streamers

### *What you need:*

- *some long streamers – make these from old sheets or other fabric, or coloured plastic carrier bags or bin liners*
- *scissors*
- *a space where you can wave the streamers*

**Ready for more?**

Tie your streamers to your fence, gate or hedge and watch them fly from inside your house.

### WHAT TO DO:

1. Make some long streamers by cutting strips of fabric, paper or plastic. Let your child help you with this.

2. Remember that your child may love cutting so much that they want to go on with this activity. If so, let them!

3. When you have several streamers, experiment together with waving them around to see which ones work best.

4. Now take your streamers to a big space indoors or outside – the garden or park is ideal.

5. Run, twirl and jump with your streamers, making patterns with them as they fly behind you.

**Another idea:** Make a simple kite from a carrier bag by tying a long string through the handles.

### DID YOU KNOW?

*Shoulder, arm and wrist muscles need to develop before fingers and hands can work.*

What is your child learning?

*Moving shoulders and arms in big movements will help your child to develop the muscles they need for writing. They will be learning how to control their arms and legs as they run, jump and twirl.*

### HELPFUL HINTS

Check to make sure the streamers are not too long, and watch for tripping or tangling.

# Down the tubes
## recycled fun

### What you need:

- *long cardboard tubes, such as those from kitchen foil*
- *toy cars that will fit down the tubes*
- *marbles, beads etc to slide down the tube*
- *a basket for the objects*
- *sticky tape or masking tape*

### WHAT TO DO:

1. If the tubes are short, tape some together to make a longer one.

2. Now sit with your child and look together down the tube.

3. Tip the objects out of the basket and take turns to slide one down the tube.

4. Try holding the tube at different angles to make objects travel more slowly or quicker.

5. Change the game by saying 'Ready, steady, go!' before you let go of the object.

6. Now take turns to tell the other one what to post down the tube – a yellow car, a red button, the red post van, the big blue marble.

**Another idea:** Collect some natural objects to slide down the tube – conkers, stones, twigs.

### Ready for more?

Have a race with two cars or two marbles and see which one comes out of the tube first or goes furthest. Put an empty tin at the bottom!

Tape more tubes together so you have a really long tunnel. You could even make corners and turns. Now roll objects down the long tunnel.

What is your child learning?

*Simple technical and scientific experiments like this are very good for children who are moving into school. If you play these exploration games with your child, they will have a head start in scientific thinking and experiment.*

### HELPFUL HINTS

Practise 'Ready, steady, go' with your child to help them wait for a starting signal.

Younger children may find a bigger tube and tennis balls easier to manage.

# Pets' parlour
## looking after pets

**What you need:**

- some soft toy pets – dogs, cats, rabbits, mice
- bowls
- brushes
- pet toys such as small balls
- some cardboard boxes for beds
- small pieces of fabric for bedding

**WHAT TO DO:**

1. Sit together with the toys and equipment.

2. Choose a pet each and talk about what they eat and drink.

3. Make some pretend food from scraps of paper or dry pasta. Put some water in a bowl for them.

4. Now talk about other things your pet needs – how you are looking after them as you brush them or make a bed for them in a box with a blanket.

5. Find some string or wool to take dogs for a pretend walk.

6. Make or find a toy for the pet, or decorate them for a party by tying ribbons in their hair or making them a special collar.

**Another idea:** Make a fish tank in a plastic box, and hang some fish on strings from the lid.

**Ready for more?**

Make an Animal Hospital for your pets. Look on the internet for pictures of animal hospitals and vets at work.

Look on the internet for advice on keeping pets. Try RSPCA.org or PDSA.org for information leaflets on all sorts of pets.

What is your child learning?

*Looking after animals is a good way to learn about looking after another person. It gives children simple rules for being kind and caring.*

### HELPFUL HINTS

Help your child to handle the toys carefully. Some children find it difficult to pretend and need you to model and support the behaviour needed.

Use this game as a way to talk about being careful when you meet animals, but not being fearful.

# Smile please
## playing with photos

***What you need:***

- *old or toy cameras*
- *some hats, sunglasses, scarves*
- *magazines with photos of people*
- *your own photo albums or collections*

WHAT TO DO:

1. Children love taking pretend photos as practice before using a real camera. Explain to your child that the camera is a toy, not one that makes real photos.

2. Play a game of photographing each other using different expressions, doing different poses, wearing the hats, glasses etc.

3. Now look in the magazines for photos of people. Tear these out and talk about them, sort them into men, women, children, babies etc. Look at the expressions – do the people look happy? sad? cross? tired? How do you know?

4. Now look at your own photo collection. Who can you find?

5. Look at some photos of your child as a baby. They will love this and want to know all the details of what they were like and what they did.

   **Another idea:** Make a photo book of just your child – either in a real album or on your computer. They will love looking at themselves from baby onwards.

**Ready for more?**

Use your mobile phone or a simple digital camera to take photos of each other.

## HELPFUL HINTS

If your child finds it difficult to recognise expressions in others, try some mirror play where they can see themselves making faces and feel the expression at the same time.

If you are considering buying a children's camera, look for one with double handles, which they will find easier to use.

What is your child learning?

*Recognising expressions is crucial to social behaviour, enabling children to understand and respond to others appropriately. It takes some children several years to reliably recognise themselves in photos and mirrors.them to learn.*

# Can you find it?
## moving on from naming

**What you need:**

- some familiar objects such as small toys, kitchen objects, a cup, a plastic bottle, a book, a pen etc.
- a box, tray or basket

**WHAT TO DO:**

1. Put all the objects in the container and sit with your child. You could sit on the settee with the box between you or on the floor.

2. Look at all the objects, taking them out and putting them back, talking about what is in the collection.

3. Now tell your child that you are going to give them a challenge to find one of the objects without you saying its name.

4. Ask them to give you something by describing its size, shape, colour, texture, use, or where it is found. Here are some examples:
   - Can you find me something round and blue? (a ball)
   - Can you find me something you find in the kitchen? (a dishcloth)
   - Can you find me something you can see through? (a bottle)

5. Praise them as they think and select objects.

**Ready for more?**

Collect some objects from your home and challenge your child to put them back in the right places.

### HELPFUL HINTS

Some children may need more help. If so, give them more clues to the object, without saying the name.

Make sure the room is distraction free – turn the TV or radio off!

What is your child learning?

*Adjectives or describing words are useful tools for children to learn. They don't need a grammar lesson, just lots of practice in using words to describe things and places, colours and shapes.*

## HELPFUL HINTS

Some children get claustrophobic under a sheet. Go under with them to give them confidence. Or give them a torch.

**What is your child learning?**

*This activity is good for physical development and for encouraging exploration and spatial awareness. Developing the story will stimulate creativity.*

# Over, under, on
## a search under the sheet

**DID YOU KNOW?**

Games such as this use 'higher order thinking skills' which are much more complex.

*What you need:*

- a sheet or duvet cover
- some toy cars or small figures
- a cardboard box for a garage
- a 'bridge' made from books or bricks and a chopping board

**WHAT TO DO:**

*This game will give your child practice in using position words such as behind, under, in, beside, on top etc.*

1. Help your child to make the bridge and place the box on its side. Now cover the bridge and the box with the sheet.

2. Ask your child to choose a vehicle or a figure.

3. Tell them you are going to put the car or figure somewhere under the sheet and they will need to go under the sheet to look for it. Now carefully go under the sheet and hide the vehicle in a definite place, e.g. under the bridge.

4. When you have hidden the object your child must go under the sheet to find it. When they have found it, they must tell you where it was.

5. Play again with a different toy in a different place.

**Another idea:** This is a good game to play on a real bed. It takes real control not to bounce!

**Ready for more?**

You hide the toy, your child goes under the sheet, finds the toy, but must leave it and just tell you where it was. This is much more difficult.

Make more structures under the sheet, in a big cardboard carton, a pop up tent or tunnel.

23

What is your
child learning?

*Careful watching
and following
instructions are
essential learning
skills.*

### DID YOU KNOW?

Using movements and words together builds stronger links in the brain.

# Follow me, follow you
## copying movements and sounds

### What you need:

- *no special equipment*

### WHAT TO DO:

1. Sit or stand opposite your child, and invite them to play 'Follow Me'.

2. When you begin this game, you need to model the leader role, but once they get the idea, your child will love to take your place, with you copying them.

3. Start by making some simple movements for your child to copy – putting your hands on your head, closing your eyes, holding your ears, poking out your tongue etc. Make these easy to copy until your child understands the game.

4. Gradually start to make more complicated movements – kneeling on one knee, putting one hand on your head and one on your knee.

5. Stop when your child loses interest.

**Another idea:** Add some words such as 'My hand is on my head' 'I'm kneeling on one knee' and ask your child to repeat this as they copy your movement.

### Ready for more?

If your child really gets good at this game, you could just play with verbal instructions such as 'Put one hand on your head and one on your foot' 'kneel on both knees and put your forehead on the floor' 'hold four fingers in the air and spin round'.

What is your child learning?

*Your child is learning a lot about you as you play this game. They are beginning to understand that their achievements are important to you, and this is vital to their wellbeing.*

DID YOU
**KNOW?**
*High self esteem releases 'feel good' chemicals in the body and brain.*

# Yes I can!
## building confidence

*What you need:*
- *no special equipment*

**WHAT TO DO:**

*Every child needs to feel capable and this activity will build their confidence. Watch your child carefully every day, so you can be both realistic and rewarding.*

**1.** Sit together somewhere comfortable. (Switch the TV and radio off so there are no distractions.)

**2.** Sing these words over and over to the tune of Twinkle, Twinkle, Little Star – *'I can do it, yes I can!'*

**3.** When you get to the end of the tune, take turns to say something the child can do – 'I can clean my teeth myself' 'You can pick up all your toys' 'You can ride your bike to the park' 'I can eat up all my tea' etc. You can use the same tune, and say the words again and again, or just say the words.

**5.** Try to reinforce things the child can already do as well as new achievements.

**6.** Finish with a hug or a 'high five' and 'I am so proud of you!'

**Another idea:** Make a photo book of your child's achievements – either in a real album or on your computer.

**Ready for more?**

Send some 'I Can' photos to grandparents and other relatives.

### HELPFUL HINTS

Some children find it really difficult to identify things they can do. These children may be late developers in self knowledge, and they need more practice. Try telling them every time they do something new – 'You just spread your own sandwich, I'm proud of you!'

Some children have low self esteem. If you think your child is one of these, make special efforts to recognise their achievements and talk about them.

## HELPFUL HINTS

If your child can't recognise or name the objects in the photos, take them to find the real thing, and take some photos of things they will recognise, such as their favourite toys.

Remember that computer time should be limited for young children. Play this game in short sessions.

# What does that do?
## looking at familiar objects

*What you need:*

- *a camera and printer or computer*

### Ready for more?

When you have looked at the pictures, ask your child if they can find the photo by asking 'Can you find the photo of the thing that boils water/ the thing that you can ride on/ the thing that you can talk to Grandma on?'

Take some more photos, but this time just photograph part of the object. See if your child can guess what the object is.

**WHAT TO DO:**

1. Walk round your home and take some pictures of familiar objects such as the fridge, a bed, the toaster, a toothbrush. Start with about six objects.

2. Print the photos or load them onto your computer.

3. Now sit with your child and look at the first picture.

4. Ask them what the object is called, and what it does. Talk together about the object, where it belongs, who it belongs to, what it is made from etc.

5. Now move on to the next photo, stopping when your child has had enough.

   **Another idea:** Use Google Images to find photos.

What is your child learning?

*Matching objects and pictures will help your child with using books, drawing and writing. Listen to their explanations of what objects do and are for, and give them praise for thinking. Being able to talk about the way things work and what they do encourages more complex language and thinking skills.*

# Paint all over
## painting dolls and toys

**What is your child learning?**

*Any painting activity will help with creativity and with fine motor control.*

### What you need:

- *newspaper or an old sheet to cover a surface in your kitchen*
- *aprons and a tray*
- *a selection of dolls, superhero characters or small world models*
- *paint brushes and cotton buds*
- *colours to paint the toys such as: pots of children's paint or finger paint, old lipsticks,*
- *flour and water mixed with food colouring, baby powder, tomato ketchup*

### WHAT TO DO:

1. Talk with your child about the game you are going to play, and let them help you to collect objects to paint. Discuss the objects they choose and make sure they are water and paint proof!

2. Put on your aprons and mix the paints together. Make sure they are thick enough to stick on the toys.

3. When the paints are ready, have some fun painting the toys. Use paintbrushes of cotton buds, and talk about the colours you are using.

4. When each toy is painted put it to dry on the tray.

5. When all the toys are done, or your child has had enough, have some fun washing the pots and brushes in warm bubbly water.

**Another idea:** Washing the toys at bath time is a great way to return them to their original colours when your child has finished with them.

### Ready for more?

Try painting a whole doll and then washing her clean again!

### DID YOU KNOW?

Transforming things is a fascination for some children. Repeated behaviour is called a schema.

### HELPFUL HINTS

Children with less advanced hand control may just want to paint the toys with their hands and fingers.

Talk all the time about parts of toys and dolls – arm, finger, leg, wheel, roof etc. to reinforce names of parts.

### HELPFUL HINTS

Some children find glue really difficult to manage. Help them without taking over. A damp cloth is always a useful thing to have handy for sticky fingers!

If your child finds it difficult to think of things for their puppet to say, help by telling a story so they only have to move the puppet around.

DID YOU **KNOW?**
Using puppets is a great way of encouraging children to talk.

# Sock it to them!
## make a simple puppet

### *What you need:*

- *some socks (adult or child size)*
- *two buttons for each puppet*
- *coloured paper or felt*
- *wool or cotton wool*
- *felt pens*
- *scissors*
- *glue stick or fabric glue*

### WHAT TO DO:

1. Talk about what you are going to do and let your child choose a sock from your collection.

2. Try the sock on and show your child how to push some of the end of the sock inside to make a mouth.

3. Keep the sock on and make two marks near the child's knuckles for the eyes. Help your child to glue on buttons for eyes.

4. Now make a nose and mouth for your puppet. The mouth should be inside the tucked in part of the sock. You could add a long tongue.

5. Stick on some lengths of wool for hair. Keep trying the puppet on to check how it looks.

6. Make a puppet for yourself so you can do a puppet play.

**Another idea:** Try making puppets from other things – gloves, mittens, the legs of tights, jumper sleeves.

What is your child learning?

*Watch your child as they use the puppet and listen for the language they use as they pretend to be someone else. This ability is a great skill and will help your child to understand others.*

**Ready for more?**

Make some more puppets and involve the whole family in the fun!

# Going shopping
## make a shop in your kitchen

*What you need:*

- *food packets and tins*
- *a flat surface for a counter and checkout*
- *a toy till or money box*
- *purses, baskets, carrier bags*
- *old credit cards and some money*
- *an adult shirt for an overall*

WHAT TO DO:

1. Help your child to set up the 'shop' in your kitchen or living room. Put the tins and packets on a shelf or arrange them on the floor.

2. Arrange a place for the checkout person to sit, and put their till or money box nearby.

3. Now talk about who is going to be the shopkeeper and who is doing the shopping. The shopkeeper wears the shirt.

4. If you are the shopper, talk about what you are doing and the things you need, thinking aloud as you collect things in a basket or bag.

5. Now go to the checkout and let your child 'ring up' the shopping on the till. Help each other to pack the shopping in a bag. Pay with money or a credit card.

**Another idea:** Try a fruit and vegetable stall, a chemist's shop or a toyshop for a change. Children love all sorts of shopping.

### Ready for more?

It's fun to be different people as you shop – and elderly customer who needs help, a mother with a baby in a pushchair, even a bad tempered person who grumbles!

### HELPFUL HINTS

If your child gets frustrated or confused, make the shop less complicated. You don't need many items to make a good shop.

Help with the language of shopping, but give plenty of time for them to think before taking over.

What is your child learning?

*The language you use as you play is a model for your child. Your child needs to learn the words and sentences adults use, and playing shops is one way to begin.*

DID YOU
KNOW?

*Almost all the maths that adults do after they leave school is connected with shopping!*

# Boxing games
## role play and imagination

### What you need:

- an empty box, big enough for your child to get inside (if you can get in too, it will be even more fun)
- sticky tape (masking tape is easy to tear, and silver duct tape is very strong, try to have both)
- felt pens

### WHAT TO DO:

*This activity is one that benefits from extra children, so invite a friend to play.*

1. Leave the box around and see what your child does with it. They will probably get inside first and may then use it as a den. In this case, you need to do little more – except perhaps to offer some picnic food or other items for the play.

2. If your child needs some help, you could suggest some ideas for making the box into a bus, car, rocket, cave, castle, house, boat etc. Then help them to cut doors and windows, castle tops etc.

3. If your child wants a companion for their play, you can provide another character, be the engine for the boat or just the provider of ideas for improving the creation.

**Another idea:** Add some thin fabrics so your child can cover openings or make curtains and flags. Smaller boxes inside the big one can become tables, desks, furniture, beds etc.

### Ready for more?

Encourage your child to decorate their space with felt pens or paints.

Open the ends of several boxes and tape them together to make a tunnel to crawl through.

### DID YOU KNOW?

*Being near your child, even if they are playing independently helps them learn.*

## HELPFUL HINTS

Some children will need help in thinking of things to make from the box. Give them some ideas, but don't take over.

Put the box on its side and tape a piece of net curtain or other thin fabric over the opening to make den. Some children will love just sitting inside, watching what is going on outside.

### What is your child learning?

*Your child is learning to think creatively and use simple recycled materials to make models, dens and other play spaces.*

# Book four

# My you have grown!
## make a growth chart

### *What you need:*

- *a long piece of paper – wallpaper is ideal, get an odd roll from a DIY store*
- *felt pens, paints*
- *stickers or other decorations*
- *blutack or other tacky material*

### WHAT TO DO:

**1.** Explain to your child that you are going to measure how tall they are and make a chart for measuring how much they are growing.

**2.** Put a long length of paper on a hard floor and weight it down with food cans.

**3.** Draw a line across the paper near one end.

**4.** Ask your child to put one of their feet with the heel on the line at the end of the paper. Draw round their foot.

**5.** Move their foot to the top of the first foot shape and draw another foot. Continue drawing heel-to-toe feet up the side of the paper till you get to the top.

**6.** Let your child lie down on the paper with their feet on the bottom line. Mark where the top of their head comes.

**7.** Put their name, age and the number of 'feet' high, on the line where their head came.

**8.** Decorate your chart with paint, felt pens and stickers, colouring in all the foot shapes.

**9.** Put the height chart on the wall where you won't forget it. Measure your child frequently but not too often!

**Another idea:** Get the rest of the family to measure themselves and put their names and the date on the chart. Remember to ask the owner of the chart for permission before writing on their chart.

### Ready for more?

Mark inches or centimetres along the opposite side of the chart from the feet. Use this to measure too.

Talk about why some people are tall and some are short. Invite your child's friends to use the chart too, but ask your child first.

## HELPFUL HINTS

This activity takes some time, and you may need to do it over more than one day, stopping when your child has had enough.

Some children are conscious of their height, be sensitive to shorter or taller than average children.

What is your child learning?

*Your child is learning about their body and simple measuring skills. Watch as they count the number of 'feet' tall they are now, and look at the chart regularly with them to check on growth.*

### DID YOU KNOW?

Some of the most famous people in history have been shorter than average!

**What is your child learning?**

*Puppet play gives children a chance to pretend to be other people. This is very important in helping them to develop understanding and empathy.*

# Who are you?
## puppet play with faces

**DID YOU KNOW?**
*Playing with puppets will help your child to understand others.*

### What you need:

- small paper plates
- chopsticks or short plant sticks
- felt pens or pictures of faces cut from magazines
- glue stick
- sticky tape

### WHAT TO DO:

1. Talk about making some masks. Look at the magazines to help decide what masks to make.

2. Help your child to make the masks with the paper plates and other resources. Draw the faces with felt pens or cut some from magazines and stick them on. Make ears, whiskers or hair from wool or raffia. Use your imagination and things you have handy to decorate your masks.

3. Tape each mask to a stick.

4. Make more puppets if your child wants to continue. You could make a range of different puppets of animals and people.

5. Now use some of the puppets you have made to talk to each other or tell a story.

6. Experiment with different voices and animal sounds.

**Another idea:** Use your puppets to re-tell a familiar story.

### Ready for more?

Do a puppet show for other members of the family or grandparents. You could sit behind the settee and hold your puppets above the settee back.

# In you go
## bath time for dolls

### What you need:

- some dolls or superhero/TV figures
- bubble bath
- flannels and towels
- a washing up bowl or baby bath (or you could use the sink)
- aprons

**Ready for more?**

Offer your child a bucket of soapy water and a washing up brush to wash trikes, toy cars, scooters and doll's pushchairs – Out of doors of course!

### WHAT TO DO:

1. Suggest to your child that it is time for the dolls or superheroes to have a bath.

2. Talk about what you need – and remember how important it is to listen to your child's suggestions.

3. Collect the things for the bath and run some warm water into the bath.

4. Now let your child add some bubble bath to the water.

5. Take any clothing off the dolls and watch as your child baths and cleans their toys.

6. Help them by commenting on what they are doing and reminding them of how to care for the toys; 'Don't forget to wash their ears' 'Be careful not to get soap in their eyes', etc.

7. After the bath, help your child to lift the toys from the water and dry them carefully.

**Another idea:** Children love water play, let them wash toys, dolls or Lego.

What is your child learning?

*The warm water and bubbles will be calming, reducing stress and making learning easier during the activity and afterwards. Your child will also be learning about looking after others and caring.*

### HELPFUL HINTS

A small bowl and toy cars is sometimes a more manageable way to offer this activity.

Use this activity to help your child to learn the names of body parts such as knees, elbows, neck etc.

# Topping fun!
## make pizzas together

**What you need:**

- some small pizza bases
- tomato puree
- toppings – grated and sliced cheese, sliced tomatoes, mushrooms, chopped ham, herbs, sliced peppers, tinned tuna, sliced onion, etc.
- small knives (not too sharp) and spoons
- bowls for toppings

**WHAT TO DO:**

*Making your own pizza is a favourite activity for young children. Apart from having the freedom to choose toppings, they get something to eat at the end!*

1. Let your child help to chop, slice and grate the toppings and put them in the bowls. Remember to offer a wide range of toppings, not just the ones they like. Children will often try something new in their own cooking.

2. Take a pizza base each and spread tomato puree all over it.

3. Now pile on your favourite toppings, remembering to sprinkle some cheese on the top. Try not to take over your child's cooking, and respect the fact that they may only choose one topping.

4. Bake your pizzas while you clear up the mess you have made!

5. Eat and enjoy.

**Another idea:** Involve your child in simple cooking tasks as you prepare meals together. They can grate, chop, sprinkle, roll, mix and stir. Use their help and have fun cooking together!

**Ready for more?**

Use French bread to make French Bread Pizzas by adding a variety of toppings and putting them under the grill.

Encourage your child to make their own sandwiches, butter their own toast, or mix their own drinks.

### HELPFUL HINTS
Some children it difficult to make choices. Limit the choice of toppings at first, then gradually increase the range. Use 'hand over hand' methods (your hand over theirs) to help with spreading and cutting, rather than doing it for them.

## DID YOU KNOW?

Cutting vegetables is much easier if you spike a fork in the vegetable and hold the fork as you cut.

## What is your child learning?

*Your child is learning how to make choices and live with the outcomes. Model the willingness to try something new yourself, even if you find you don't like it! You are a powerful model and teacher for your child.*

DID YOU KNOW?

*Confidence releases chemicals in the brain that will have a calming effect on your child.*

# What's inside?
## talking about what things are for

### What you need:

- two or three cloth bags
- two or three small collections of objects such as:
  - a toy phone, a pen and a notepad
  - a screwdriver, some screws and a piece of wood
  - bubble bath, a sponge and some pyjamas
  - an empty washing up liquid bottle, a cloth, and plastic cutlery
  - a toy, some wrapping paper and a gift tag

### Ready for more?

Make some collections of objects for different people – Dad's newspaper, comb, socks, phone; or Mum's makeup bag, purse, magazine; or a baby bag with a nappy, baby brush, sippy cup.

### WHAT TO DO:

1. Put each collection in a separate bag.

2. Put the bags in a pile.

3. Let your child choose one of the bags and tip the contents on the floor or table.

4. Talk about the objects and what they are for, demonstrating what you do with each.

5. Put the objects back in the bag and choose another one.

6. Carry on looking at the bags until your child has had enough.

**Another idea:** When you have finished the game, play a new game of finding the right place for all the things from the bags and putting them away.

### What is your child learning?

*Using describing words may be a new stage for your child. Describing what things do and the relationship between a group of objects needs more complex thinking and speaking skills. Encourage your child to expand their vocabulary into sentences by asking simple questions and speaking in sentences yourself.*

### HELPFUL HINTS

Some children need more thinking time than others. Allow plenty of time for exploring the objects before starting to talk.

You may need to model or mime the uses of some objects so your child can link the objects with actions.

# Hunt the sound
## a new take on Hunt the Thimble

**What you need:**

- *a kitchen timer, alarm clock with a loud tick or transistor radio with the sound turned down very low.*

**WHAT TO DO:**

1. Turn off the television or radio.

2. Invite your child to play 'Hunt the sound' with you, and show them the sound maker you have chosen for the game.

3. Now explain how to play. One person hides the clock, timer or other sound maker and the other player must find it by listening very carefully.

4. Decide who will go first. The 'finder' must cover their eyes or go into another room. The 'hider' hides the sound maker.

5. Now the 'finder' must listen for the sound. The 'hider' can say 'warmer' or 'colder' to help as the 'finder' walks around the room looking for the object.

6. When the 'finder' has found the object, swap roles for the next turn.

What is your child learning?

*Any listening games that you play will help your child to learn to speak fluently and learn to read more easily.*

**Ready for more?**

Play listening games out of doors. Recall some of the games you played as a child, such as 'Grandma's Footsteps', 'Blind Man's Buff' or 'What's the Time Mr Wolf?'.

### HELPFUL HIINTS

When your child first plays this game, you may need to walk with them as they search, encouraging them to stop and listen for the sound.

When you play as a family, you could play in pairs, and adult and a child together.

DID YOU **KNOW?**
*Most girls' hearing is better than boys' throughout life.*

### HELPFUL HINTS

Help your child with mixing and painting, but try not to take over.

Test the bottles first and choose ones that are easy to squeeze.

### DID YOU KNOW?

*Messy, hands-on activities make children's brains more active.*

# Paint it puffy
## textured painting

**What is your baby learning?**

*What you need:*

- *flour and water*
- *salt*
- *paint or food colouring*
- *clean empty washing up liquid bottles or water bottles with drinking tops*
- *a cup or small mug*
- *a bowl*
- *a funnel*
- *some thick paper or card*

### WHAT TO DO:

1. Help your child to make two or more colours of puffy paint by mixing the following in your bowl for each colour
   - 1 cup flour
   - 1 cup salt
   - 1 cup water
   - enough paint or food colouring to make the colour you want

2. Mix the paint thoroughly and pour it into a bottle.

3. Make more colours till you have as many as you want.

4. Put the tops on the bottles and turn them upside down to paint. Let your child make wiggles and patterns on the card or paper. Watch what the paint does as it comes out of the bottles.

5. As the paint dries it will puff up and make a raised pattern.

**Another idea:** Try this paint out of doors on a fine day, and let your child use a hose to wash it off later.

*Watching and talking about how things change are important ways to encourage scientific thinking. You don't need to know why the paint puffs up, just talk with your child about what is happening, and what makes this paint different from other paints. The secret is in the flour, but see if they can work out what's different!*

### Ready for more?

Make big quantities by doubling the recipe and use these for really big paintings on rolls of wallpaper.

DID YOU
KNOW?
*Girls are generally
better at distinguishing
and naming colours
than boys.*

# Sort it!
## laundry fun

**What is your child learning?**

*Sorting and matching are mathematical activities, whether it's sorting Lego bricks into colours, lining up cars in colour groups, matching socks or gloves. Your child is learning about relationships between objects, and this will give their mathematical brain a boost.*

**What you need:**
- a full laundry basket
- a space for sorting

**WHAT TO DO:**

1. Talk to your child about the game and explain why you need to sort the washing before putting it in the washing machine.

3. Put one piece of washing of each colour on the floor round the laundry basket. Show your child how to take one piece of clothing at a time from the laundry basket and put it on the pile for each colour.

4. Talk about colours and shades, and which colours can be washed together.

5. When all the washing is sorted, let your child help you load the machine.

6. Don't forget to thank your child for helping you!

**Another idea:** When the washing is dry get your child to help you sort it into piles for each member of the family. Matching socks is a very good activity!

**Ready for more?**

Your child can help with many other household chores. This won't only make them better citizens, but will help their learning. Encourage them to help with washing and sorting containers for recycling; folding newspapers, tea towels, pillowcases; hanging up towels in the bathroom; helping to tidy their bedroom; putting shopping away pairing up shoes in the hall.

### HELPFUL HINTS

Start this activity when there is not too much washing or it will really become a chore for both of you.

Some children find colours easy, but shades harder – talk about dark, light, pale etc.

# Squeeze and decorate
## icing biscuits and buns

**What you need:**

- aprons
- shop bought or home made buns or biscuits
- icing sugar and water
- coloured icing in tubes
- cake decorations such as 'hundreds and thousands' and jelly sweets
- containers such as a bun tray or muffin tin for the the decorations
- spoons

**WHAT TO DO:**

1. Wash your hands and put on your aprons.

2. Look together at all the decorations and the buns or biscuits, and talk about how you could decorate them.

3. Help the children to mix some white icing by mixing icing sugar and a little water.

4. Show your child how to spoon some white icing onto a bun or biscuit, leaving it to spread out over the surface.

5. Now they can decorate the bun or biscuit however they choose, using the range of decorations in the containers.

6. Carefully put each finished bun or biscuit on a serving plate and do another one.

7. Do some yourself, and remember to encourage your child to show their own creativity and imagination.

**Another idea:** This is a great family activity. Try it for Christmas biscuits or party cakes.

**Ready for more?**

Let your child decorate a cake first, then you copy their pattern.

Mix coloured icing instead of white, talking about how the food colouring works to make the icing change.

HELPFUL HINTS

Talking through what your child is doing as they do it is a good way of helping them to learn.

Decorations in shakers will help some children with hand control diffculties.

DID YOU KNOW?

Making food for others is an activity that releases calming endorphins in your child's brain.

## What is your child learning?

*This is a community activity where children can make a real contribution to their family. This will give them a lot of pleasure and great motivation, Try to do some cooking with your child every week and you will teach them all sorts of life skills and useful techniques.*

### HELPFUL HINTS

If you think your child may find whole spaghetti strings really difficult to manage, break them in half before cooking them.

Help them manage the strings by supporting some of the length. Don't try to make pictures, just patterns, squiggles, spirals etc.

**What is your child learning?**

*This is another activity that combines creativity with early science. Talking about changes, feeling the textures of materials and creating their own patterns will all help your child to develop good attitudes to learning.*

# Sticky wiggles
## spaghetti magic

**DID YOU KNOW?**
Touching and talking switches on more brain cells than just watching.

### What you need:

- *some uncooked spaghetti*
- *a saucepan of water*
- *a colander or sieve*
- *a plastic box or a zip lock bag*
- *sheets of paper or card*

### WHAT TO DO:

1. Talk about what you are going to do. Let your child feel and talk about the uncooked spaghetti, describing how it feels, looks and smells.

2. Now let your child watch as you cook the spaghetti in boiling water, using the instructions on the packet. While it is cooking, get the paper ready.

3. When it is cooked, drain the spaghetti well in a colander or sieve (don't rinse it!) and put it in a bag or plastic box to cool down for handling. This will also stop the spaghetti drying out.

4. When the spaghetti is cool, help your child to lift strands and make patterns on the paper.

5. The starch in the spaghetti will make it stick like magic to the paper or card as it dries!

**Another idea:** Try the same activity with instant noodles.

### Ready for more?

Put some food colouring in a plastic bag with the cooked spaghetti to make coloured spaghetti.

# Tiny things
## fingers and thumbs

### What is your child learning?

*Pincer movement and fine motor control are important physical skills. Your child is also learning a lot about maths while they play this game. Sorting, counting and finding similarities are all mathematical concepts.*

### *What you need:*

- *some very small items – lentils, dried beans and peas, small pasta shapes, buttons, paper clips etc*
- *some containers with sections – plastic liners from biscuit or other food packaging, egg boxes, little bowls, saucers*
- *A big tray, or plant saucer*

### WHAT TO DO:

1. Choose three or four different objects to start with. Put each sort of small object in its own container and put the containers on the tray, so spilled objects are safely contained.

2. Let your child explore the objects. They will probably mix them all up, pouring, sifting and handling them to see what they are like.

3. Play with them, talking about what the objects look and feel like. Model using your first finger and thumb in a 'pincer movement' to pick up individual objects.

   **Another idea:** Collect all sorts of screws, bolts, nails, washers and nuts.

**DID YOU KNOW?**
The human brain craves order, and works tirelessly to find links and similarities.

### Ready for more?

When all the things are muddled up, have a go at sorting them all out again. Make the task achievable by just offering a few sorts of objects.

Get some plastic tweezers and try this game again. Children really like using tweezers and they are very good exercise for fingers and hands.

### HELPFUL HINTS

Limit the range of objects you offer, particularly to start with.

Choose larger objects such as dried butter beans, bigger buttons, macaroni pieces, coins. This will make sorting and picking up easier.

## HELPFUL HINTS
Offer help if your child finds it difficult to manage some of the items of clothing.

# Whacky dressing
## dress up together!

**What you need:**
- *a washing basket*
- *some adult's and children's clothing – gloves, hats, scarves, sunglasses, shoes, socks, football shorts.*

**WHAT TO DO:**

1. Explain to your child that you are going to play a funny dressing up game, called 'Find it and put it on'.

2. Sit on the floor or settee with your child and look at the clothes in the basket. Check that they know what each item is called and can say the name.

3. Now take turns to ask each other to put on an item of clothing. Use the same words each time – for example, '*Your child's name*, find a hat and put it on.' Using your child's name each time keeps them on track.

4. Keep this item of clothing on.

5. Go on asking each other to put on more clothes. It makes the game even more fun if you end up with two hats on, or trying to put shoes on when you are already wearing gloves!

6. Keep going till you can't put anything else on or you are laughing so much you can't play any more!

**Another idea:** Play this game as a whole family – it's a great celebration or party game.

**Ready for more?**

Add some silly items of clothing such as party hats, a tutu, disco headbands, a top hat, earmuffs etc.

**DID YOU KNOW?**

*Laughter and enjoyment make learning much more effective.*

What is your child learning?

*Putting clothes on is a challenge for all children, and practising it in a game is a very useful way of learning about what goes where. Taking turns in games is also a very important skill.*

# Feel like a walk?
## a 'feely' walk

### *What you need:*

- *no special equipment, just a place to walk*
- *you could take a camera or collecting bag for memories*

### WHAT TO DO:

*You can go on a 'feely' walk anywhere – indoors, in the garden, at the park, on the way to the shops, on the way back from nursery or meeting older children from school.*

1. Before you start, tell your child about 'feely' walks where you will be feeling everything and trying to find as many different surfaces as you can. If you are at the park or in the street, warn your child that some things are not good to touch, as these may be dangerous or unhealthy.

2. As you walk, touch and feel surfaces and objects, using texture words as you describe the objects – a bumpy tree trunk, a cold metal sign, a fluffy cat, a hard brick wall, a smooth stone etc.

3. If you are in a wood or field or at the park, collect some interesting natural objects to take home.

   **Another idea:** Try to talk about textures at other times – the textures of food, of toys, of clothing, of skin, nails, hair etc

### DID YOU KNOW?

Children will often be happier to do this sort of activity AFTER play.

### Ready for more?

If you have collected some objects, talk about these when you get home and see if you can sort them into groups of smooth, rough, sharp etc.

Use photos to help your child to talk to you or someone else about the walk and what you found. Use your mobile phone or download the photos to a computer.

### HELPFUL HINTS

Some children need encouragement to slow down and really use their senses. Be sensitive to your child's unique needs and find a good time for this activity.

Make some suggestions of texture words and sometimes ask your child 'Is it rough or smooth?' 'Do you think it's bumpy or rough?'

## What is your child learning?

*Every time you give your child a hands-on activity to do, they will be learning new things. If you stay with them during the activity and talk about what you are doing together, they will learn more.*

DID YOU
KNOW?
Close physical contact
with a parent releases
calming chemicals in
the brain, reducing
stress.

# Snuggle time
## a cosy time together

**What is your child learning?**

*Your child will be learning that you enjoy their company and like being quiet with them. This is particularly important for young children and helps them to become more confident and able to manage being separated from you at other times.*

### What you need:

- *a time when you will not be rushed or distracted*
- *a snuggly place to sit, such as a settee with lots of cushions, or a bed*
- *some soft toys, furry ones are best*
- *pieces or items of clothing made from soft fabrics such as fleece, fur, velvet*
- *some favourite stories (quiet, gentle ones are best*
- *some soothing music*

### WHAT TO DO:

1. Switch off any distractions such as TV or radio.

2. Invite your child for a 'Snuggle Time' with you, and settle down with all the soft and tactile things.

3. Look at all the soft toys and fabrics you have collected, stroke them and talk about them.

4. Hug and stroke your child gently. This will make them feel really relaxed and secure.

5. Now read a favourite story together. Make your voice calm and quiet as you read, so your child continues to feel relaxed.

6. Now listen to some calming music if you have a music player handy. Don't worry if you go to sleep!

**Another idea:** Have regular Snuggle Times as a family, maybe on weekend mornings or in the holidays when everyone can be more relaxed. It's important for Dads to be involved in these times too.

### Ready for more?

Bedtime toys are very important to most children at some time during their early years. Make sure you include them in Snuggle Time.

### HELPFUL HINTS

Some children find it difficult to stop and relax. A perfumed candle or aromatherapy oils will sometimes help.

**HELPFUL HINTS**

Let your child gently feel the objects through the cloth as they think about which one they are looking for.

# Peep and match
## picture and object matching

### *What you need:*

- *a collection of small familiar items such as a teddy, a cup, a brush, a spoon, a small toy animal, a glove*
- *a camera or mobile phone with a camera*
- *a tea towel or small blanket*

**Ready for more?**

Use two similar objects, two different spoons, different coloured cups, different toy cars. Take pictures of each one to make the game more difficult.

### WHAT TO DO:

1. Take a photo of each of the objects you have collected.

2. Sit with your child where they can see the objects and the photos (on your phone or camera screen or the computer).

3. Spread all the objects out on the floor or a table, and cover them with a tea-towel or small blanket.

4. Show your child one of the photos and ask them if they can peep under the cloth and find the object. If they can, they pick it up and keep it.

5. Now you have a go.

6. Carry on taking turns until all the objects have been matched.

**Another idea:** Put a few objects on a tray and look at them for a moment. Cover with a cloth. Now slide one object out from under the cloth, remove the cloth and see if your child knows what is missing.

What is your child learning?

*Some children learn better when they look at things. These children are sometimes called visual learners, and they will be able to play these games more easily. However, your child needs to learn from listening and touching as well as looking. Learning with all their senses will really help them in school and life.*

# Gloop
## more messy play

### What is your child learning?

*Your child is learning that learning is fun! They are also learning about the world about them, how materials move and the language of describing movement, materials and texture.*

**What you need:**

- a packet of cornflour
- water in a jug
- mixing bowl, spoon
- a flat tray or big plant saucer with a lip
- aprons

**WHAT TO DO:**

1. Put the cornflour in a bowl and help your child to add water slowly until the mixture is thick and not too runny, stirring all the time.

2. Carefully tip the Gloop into the tray and play with your child, lifting the Gloop and letting it run between your fingers.

3. Talk about the Gloop and the strange way it behaves. Use descriptive words to talk about the texture and how the Gloop behaves.

4. Keep playing till your child has had enough, but keep it handy as they will probably want to come back later.

**Another idea:** Add food colouring to the mixture for coloured gloop. Add it to the white mixture in the tray and swirl it round to mix it.

### Ready for more?

Make your own finger paint. Mix two tablespoons of cornflour and two tablespoons of cold water in a small saucepan. Add one cup of water and gently cook until it is as thick as custard, *stirring all the time.* Add food colouring or paint (or some aromatherapy oils) and store in the fridge after use.

### HELPFUL HINTS

Most children will need no encouragement to get involved, but if your child doesn't like getting messy, show them that you do!

Help your child to clean up spills of Gloop with old credit or debit cards. This will gve them some more hand control exercise.

### DID YOU KNOW?

Messy play is essential in building strong brains.

## What is your child learning?

*In this activity your child is learning
about the pleasure of giving to others.
Wrapping, tying and taping are all good
for fine motor skills and hand control.*

# A present for you
## parcels and gifts

### *What you need:*

- *old wrapping paper, gift wrap, tissue paper, cellophane, small gift boxes and gift bags*
- *sticky tape in a dispenser (or masking tape, which is easier for small fingers to tear)*
- *pens, scissors*
- *small toys and objects to pack*
- *some soft toys*

### WHAT TO DO:

*Young children love to wrap up toys and other objects as 'presents' for other people. The content of the parcel isn't important, the giving is!*

1. Collect together all the materials for wrapping presents, and look at them with your child.

2. Suggest that they might like to help you wrap some toys up and pretend it is Christmas or their favourite toy's birthday.

3. Decide together what you think the toy would like, and choose paper and other wrapping to wrap it in. Help them with tape or with holding the parcel while they do the tape.

4. When you have some parcels, give them to the toy or human recipient.

5. Continue till your child has had enough.

**Another idea:** Children will love to wrap their own Christmas and birthday presents for friends and family. Let them do it, and be proud of their achievements.

### Ready for more?

Your child can write their own messages in cards for family birthdays and other celebrations. Don't worry if they can only write the first letter of their name or if you need to ask them what they have written. Having a go is the important thing.

Have a Teddy Bears' Birthday party with cards, gifts and food.

### HELPFUL HINTS

Some children will need help with scissors and tape as they get better at using them. Try 'hand over hand' with scissors rather than doing it for them.

Cut some of the paper into smaller pieces and cut or tear some lengths of tape to make the wrapping easier.

## What is your child learning?

*Scientific, technological and mathematical development are all extended by experiment and trying again and again. Encourage your child to keep trying even when the tower tumbles down. Perseverance is a very desirable ability.*

### HELPFUL HINTS

Some children find this sort of building frustrating, particularly when the tower tumbles. Be patient, praise their work and tell them you understand their frustration. Keep on building.

Some children get very excited by this game, be understanding of them too as they learn to manage their excitement.

# Toppling towers
## build it high!

### DID YOU KNOW?

*Children learn about concepts of gravity, balance, size and shape by experiment.*

### *What you need:*

- *cardboard boxes and cartons – cereal boxes, shoe boxes, all sorts of packets*
- *sticky or masking tape*

### WHAT TO DO:

1. Let your child help you to tape the ends of all the boxes shut, so you can build with them. Make sure all the boxes are strong enough to balance on each other.

2. Now work with your child to make the tallest tower you can. Keep going, balancing one box on another until the tower topples.

3. Now build another one. This time count the boxes as you build.

4. Talk about why the tower falls down and what you could do to make the tower steadier and stronger.

5. Try to build a higher tower. Guess how any boxes you can use before the tower falls.

### Ready for more?

Use food cans to make towers. This is better on carpet!

Add some cardboard tubes to your towers, see if you can balance boxes on the tubes, or use the tubes for chimneys and pillars.

**Another idea:** When you go shopping, encourage your child to look at piles of cans, cartons, boxes and bottles displayed at supermarkets.

# Bows and knots
## tying and threading

### What you need:

- string, wool, ribbon
- pieces of fabric (old sheets, shirts or other clothing)
- plastic carrier bags
- a fence, bush or tree (if you haven't got a garden, buy some plastic coated garden netting and use this indoors, tied to a door frame)
- a camera

### WHAT TO DO:

1. Tear the old fabric into strips, and cut the carrier bags into more strips. Cut the string, ribbon etc onto manageable pieces.

2. Put everything into a bag and go outside with your child.

3. Show them how to tie ribbons and strips on the fence or bushes, and weave the strips in and out of spaces.

4. Have fun tying and weaving, making patterns or just adding colours as you fancy.

5. Take some photos of your creation.

6. Add some natural objects such as grasses, twigs, feathers etc to your creation.

**Another idea:** Get a piece of fishing net or garden netting made with string. Hang this up in your house and use it for a message board.

### What is your child learning?

*Fine motor skills are essential for reading, writing, typing, drawing and many other skills.*

### Ready for more?

Do some weaving with grass, flowers, leaves, hay, little sticks etc. Hammer nails on two sides of an old wooden picture frame or wooden box. Wind some string from end to end of the frame to make the warp of the weaving. Then weave natural things under and over the strings.

### HELPFUL HINTS

Some children will need help with tying. Show them how to do it, then use 'hand over hand' to help their fingers do the work.

Use plenty of praise to keep concentration going.

### DID YOU KNOW?

*Weaving and tying were traditionally used to train children's fingers and hands.*

# One for you and me
## sharing with others

### *What you need:*

- *some cooked spaghetti*
- *dry pasta shapes*
- *small spoons*
- *plates*
- *bowls*

### WHAT TO DO:

1. Cook some spaghetti, rinse it well and mix it with a little cooking oil to stop it sticking together. Put the spaghetti in a bowl.

2. Invite your child to come and join you, and perhaps bring a soft toy to play too.

3. Put the bowl of spaghetti in the middle and ask your child to give everyone a plate, including one for any visiting toys.

4. Now take turns to gently pull a strand of spaghetti for each person out of the bowl. Put it on their plate, saying 'One for you, one for you, one for me'. Continue until all the spaghetti is shared out.

5. Now bring out the dry pasta shapes and some small spoons.

6. Serve out the pasta shapes, counting 'One, two, three' as you spoon it out.

### Ready for more?

Have tea parties and picnics with dolls, teddies and other toys. Invite friends to come to tea and provide small finger food for sharing.

### What is your child learning?

*Sharing is a first step towards mathematical division. Help your child to understand sharing fairly and talk with them about what to do with any that are left over – 'What would be fair?'*

### HELPFUL HINTS

If your child finds it difficult to share among more than two people, restrict the game to the two of you, and put out less food to share.

Remember to use sharing words and counting at mealtimes and when you are shopping.

## HELPFUL HINTS

Some children find it easy to use both hands, others will need encouragement and help. Use encouragement and praise and model the actions by doing your own painting.

Some children will still be using their whole fist to grip the brush or pen. Don't worry, they will develop a more adult writing grip later. Forcing them to change their grip at this age may put them off forever!

## What is your child learning?

*Using both hands switches on both sides of the brain and encourages links between them. This sort of activity is very important for learning all sorts of skills, not just reading and writing. Frequent practice in 'both hands' activities will help them for the rest of their lives.*

# Both hands
## mark making

### What you need:

- *paper*
- *an easel and pegs or clips, OR a flat door with Blu-tack or masking tape*
- *paint*
- *chunky paint brushes*

### WHAT TO DO:

1. Fix a big piece of paper firmly to the door or easel.

3. Help your child to prepare the paints and find the brushes.

4. Now talk about a different way of painting, with two hands instead of one.

5. Let your child take a paintbrush in each hand and make patterns and shapes using both hands. Don't encourage them to paint a picture or to make both hands do the same thing. The aim of the activity is to enjoy using both together.

6. If you have space, join in by doing your own painting.

**Another idea:** Use bath paint or finger paint on the bathroom tiles, using both hands, than use the shower to clean the paint off.

### Ready for more?

Give your child a pile of bricks, pegs or buttons and two containers. Pick up one in each hand at the same time and put one in each container.

### DID YOU KNOW?

Using both hands for activities does NOT stop your child developing a dominant hand!

**HELPFUL HINTS**

If your child is finding it difficult, just play with two pairs – your shoe and theirs, and two spoons.

# Size matters!
## big one, small one

**DID YOU KNOW?**

*Organising objects in sequence is an important mathematical concept.*

*What you need:*

- *a collection of everyday objects, a big one and a small one of each – spoons, plates, cups, shoes, gloves, socks, shells, plastic containers, etc*
- *a big basket to put them in*

**WHAT TO DO:**

1. Put all the objects in the basket and mix them up.

2. Now look at the objects together, picking them up, feeling them and talking about them.

3. Take a bit of time to look at the pairs of objects in the basket.

4. Now play the 'big one, small one' game. Take turns to say the name of an object and the other player must find the matching pair.

5. When you have found all the pairs, play a game together. Tip all the objects on the floor, and race to find all the pairs and put them back in the basket.

**Another idea:** Play this game with clean washing, finding all the pairs of socks or all the clothes belonging to each family member.

**Ready for more?**

Collect some trios of objects, small, medium and large – spoons, cups, plastic bottles, clothing etc. Use this collection to play 'Find me'. Take turns to give instructions such as 'Find me the biggest spoon' 'Find me the middle sized sock'.

What is your child learning?

*This game is about thinking. The concepts of small, bigger, big and small, middle sized, big are complex and more difficult than just matching identical objects.*

# Bang it!
## drumming fun

**What is your child learning?**

*Children who learn by moving and by listening, often called kinaesthetic or auditory learners will particularly enjoy this activity. If your child finds learning by looking easier, try letting them accompany music on the television or on a DVD. Seeing the players may make it easier.*

### *What you need:*

- *washing up bowls and plastic boxes of all sizes (get cheap bowls at Pound Shops)*
- *big biscuit tins*
- *wooden spoons or chopsticks*
- *radio, CD or MP3 player for music*
- *a selection of music with a good beat*

### WHAT TO DO:

1. Collect together all the equipment for your drum band.

2. Turn the bowls, boxes and tins upside down on the ground or floor.

3. Show your child how they can use the wooden spoons as drumsticks.

4. Put on some music and play together.

5. Once your child has got the idea, they may want to play on their own, but don't go too far away, just sit nearby and be an appreciative audience!

**Another idea:** Add some saucepans and old metal cutlery to your band. Or tie some old pans on the garden fence or in the hedge for outdoor music playing.

### Ready for more?

Try making some music with plastic plates and chopsticks, keeping the beat with lively music, and tapping the stick on the plate above your head, by your feet, behind your back.

### DID YOU KNOW?

Being able to keep a steady beat is essential to learning to read.

### HELPFUL HINTS

Help your child to play in time by using 'hand over hand' methods, holding their hand under yours as you play together.

Some children don't like loud music or noises. If so, tie some fabric round the end of the wooden spoons to soften the sound.

## HELPFUL HINTS

Some children may need extra encouragement to persevere with the activity till they have found all the treasure. Use praise and encouragement to keep them going, and weave a made up story round the game.

Dressing up first sometimes encourages children to really engage in the activity. Try starting with some dressing up, or reading a pirate story.

# Buried treasure
## a hide and find game

**What you need:**

- a tray or big bowl of sand
- silver and gold buttons
- plastic coins
- pretend 'gems' and glass 'nuggets'
- shells and pretty stones
- small bowls, yogurt pots or egg boxes

**WHAT TO DO:**

1. Before you start, secretly fill the bowl or tray with sand and hide all the treasure in it.

2. Now tell your child that there is some treasure buried in the bowl and you need some help to find it all.

3. Ask them how you could make sure that you find everything, and take their suggestions for utensils or tools you could use.

4. Now help each other to find all the treasure in the bowl and sort it into the different pots.

5. Talk about all the things as you find them.

6. Ask your child who they think the treasure belongs to, and encourage them to be imaginative abut where it might have come from and if you should try to find the owner.

**DID YOU KNOW?**

Children with creative minds will do better at school.

**Ready for more?**

If your child wants to give the treasure back, you could write a letter together to the pirate or other owner. Or you could make a poster. It's even better fun if your child gets a reply!

Make eye patches, tie scarves round your heads and invite some of your child's friends to a Pirate Party.

**Another idea:** Play treasure hunts around your home or in the garden. Don't forget to have an Easter Egg hunt with little eggs hidden in all sorts of surprising places!

**What is your child learning?**

*This activity is helping to develop your child's creative thinking and language skills.*

**DID YOU KNOW?**

*Walking around while you play shakers with both hands makes the brain work even harder.*

# Make and shake
## make and play a simple shaker

*What you need:*
- *some small plastic water bottles (washed and dried thoroughly)*
- *small dry items, such as rice, small dry pasta shapes, little buttons*
- *strong tape or glue*
- *a funnel*

**Ready for more?**

Make some tin shakers from film canisters (get these from camera shops). Fill them with different things and play a guessing game as you listen to the sounds they make.

**WHAT TO DO:**

1. Let your child help to collect the things you need, and show them how you can make a funnel from a washing up liquid bottle.

2. Talk about what you are going to do, and explain how to make a shaker.

3. Now help your child to choose what they will put in their shaker.

4. Use the funnel to put some of the chosen items in an empty bottle. Don't fill it too full – about one third full is plenty.

5. Screw the top on the bottle and try it to see how it works. Use tape to stick the lid firmly on to the bottle.

6. Make a shaker for yourself, and try to make it sound different from your child's.

7. Now have a shaker band together as you listen to some music.

What is your child learning?

*This activity will help to improve your child's listening and concentration skills. If you play together, turn taking will stretch their listening and turn taking abilities.*

# Paint magic
## try some different ways of painting

**What you need:**
- *paper or card from packaging*
- *plastic medicine droppers*
- *cotton buds*
- *straws*
- *paint in several colours, bun tray or small pots*

**WHAT TO DO:**

1. Help your child to make some runny paint by adding water to finger paint or poster paint.

2. Now work with your child to experiment with the runny paint, using droppers, straws, cotton buds etc. The paint should be runny enough to drip and drop onto the surface of the paper.

3. Gently tip the paper or card to make the paint run down and across the painting.

4. Talk about what is happening to the paint as you work. Look at each other's creations.

5. When the painting is finished, put it somewhere flat to dry and try another one.

**Another idea:** Use some big sheets of paper for drippy paintings and use these as personalised wrapping paper, or paint on white card and cut it up to make greeting cards or gift tags.

### DID YOU KNOW?
When children are interested and enjoying an activity, they will learn more.

### Ready for more?
Try mixing the paint with condensed milk or white glue and add water to make it runny. This will make shiny paint.

Add washing up liquid to runny paint, put it in yogurt pots and blow with a straw to make bubbles. Put a piece of paper over the top of the pot to make a bubble print.

### HELPFUL HINTS
Some children are still developing hand control, so they may find it difficult to make the paint do what they want. Help them to persevere, it will really help them.

Dripping, dropping, blowing and tipping are messy activities, be patient and work in the kitchen!

### What is your child learning?

*Enjoyable, creative activities like this are very good for improving hand-eye coordination and concentration.*

What is your child learning?

*Learning about the environment and growing things is essential for all children.*

# Mashers, mud pies
## messy play out of doors

### What you need:

* a garden or other space outside with one or more of the following:
* a bucket of water and a decorating brush
* a sand box
* a place to make mud pies
* big chalks
* some simple tools such as spades and buckets, watering can, potato masher, whisk, hand spray, small trowel

### WHAT TO DO:

*Children really benefit from being outside every day, so each morning, look outside and decide what you could do together in your outside space. Here are some ideas:*

1. Make mud pies in a muddy puddle.

2. Fill a bucket with water and 'paint' the walls, patio or windows with water.

3. Use a window scraper to scrape rain from the windows.

4. Spray a mixture of water and food colouring water from a hand spray on a sheet or shower curtain hung outside.

**Another idea:** Feed the birds – use bread or bird seed, or thread peanuts (in their shells) on a string to hang in a tree.

### Ready for more?

Get involved in simple gardening with your child. Plant some seeds in pots or grow lettuce, carrots or tomatoes in a grow bag or pots.

### HELPFUL HINTS

Some children get so used to being indoors that they resist going out. Encourage them by doing interesting things out of doors.

Riding bikes, scooters, roller skating, pushing a doll's pushchair, collecting things in a little bag, even putting on an explorer's rucksack may inspire your child to come outside with you.

# Freezer fun
## use your freezer for learning

**What you need:**

- *an ice cube tray*
- *a jug of cold water*
- *a selection of fruit juices or freshly squeezed juice*
- *cocktail cherries or small pieces of fruit (optional)*
- *spoons*
- *small jugs*
- *drinking glasses*

**WHAT TO DO:**

1. Announce to your child that it is 'Cocktail Time' and invite them to join you for cocktail making.

2. Collect all the things you need and set them out where you can both see and reach them. Explain that you are going to make cocktail ice cubes first.

3. Now help your child to choose a fruit juice and pour a little in the small jug.

4. If they want to mix the juices, add another flavour to the jug and stir to mix.

5. Put cherries or other fruit pieces in each ice cube compartment.

6. Help your child to spoon some juice into each compartment and top up with water.

7. Freeze and enjoy in fruit juice, cordial or even water.

**Another idea:** Make different flavours in the tray, and try some of more exotic juices such as pineapple, guava, kiwi or mango.

### DID YOU KNOW?
Pouring and spooning liquids is a very good way of improving hand-eye coordination.

### Ready for more?
Use a liquidiser to make your own smoothies and milk shakes. Mix berries and milk, add some ice cubes and whiz together in a liquidiser to make a healthy drink with no added sugar.

## HELPFUL HINTS

Some children don't like very cold drinks, or will only drink one type of juice. Respect this, but try to encourage them to accept a wider range of foods and drinks.

Help with spooning and pouring by using 'hand over hand' help with your hand over theirs. Try not to take over.

## What is your child learning?

*This activity gives good practice for hand-eye coordination.*

# Assault course
## use that energy!

**What you need:**

- blankets and sheets
- small pieces of furniture
- cushions
- clothes pegs and string

**WHAT TO DO:**

*This activity is very good for the sort of day when energy levels are high and you can't take your child outside to work it off. It will keep you in control while they do something physical.*

### DID YOU KNOW?

*Physical activity reduces stress and helps everyone to feel calmer!.*

### Ready for more?

Find somewhere free from danger and see how many times your child can do head over heels, jump on and off a cushion, throw a rolled pair of socks into a bowl, jump to reach high up a wall, even do press-ups.

1. Suggest to your child that you could make an assault or commando course.

2. Decide together where the best and safest place would be. You might use the garage, a spare bedroom, your child's bedroom or even your living room if you can child-proof it!

3. Work together to organise a course that involves all sorts of challenges such as crossing rivers on stepping stone cushions or crawling under blankets.

What is your child learning?

### HELPFUL HINTS

This activity is good for children who get frustrated when they can't rush about. The control is good for them and for you.

Adapt the course to meet your child's ability and maturity, don't make it too difficult or they will lose interest. The idea is to have fun and work off some energy.

*In this activity your child is learning how to control their movements in a structured way. They are also learning that you understand their need for physical activity every day.*

**HELPFUL HINTS**
If your child is scared of the dark, put a light in the dark place before you go in and always stay with them.

What is your child learning?

*This safe activity will give your child confidence about the dark and help them to take control of their fears.*

# Lighting up time!
## fun with torches

**DID YOU KNOW?**
*Light levels are so high in most places that children often have no experience of real darkness.*

**What you need:**
- a sheet or blanket, or a dark place such as the cupboard under the stairs
- cushions
- one or two torches
- battery powered lights, flashing light toys
- a string of battery powered Christmas lights (optional)

**WHAT TO DO:**

1. Look under beds, in wardrobes, in the airing cupboard until you find somewhere dark that fits you.

2. Take some cushions, torches and other lights into your dark place.

3. Talk about how some people are scared of the dark, and that they don't need to be. Be aware of any fears your chid has and talk about these.

4. Experiment with flashing and coloured lights and talk about what it's like to be in the dark together. If they feel brave enough, switch the lights off for a moment to see how dark it is.

5. Ask your child if they know the names of any animals that come out in the dark, and why they sleep in the daytime. See if you can find any toy animals or birds to live in your dark place.

**Another idea:** Find some stories about the dark or night time.

**Ready for more?**

Go on a night walk with torches and flashlights. What can you see?

# Take care
## a safety game

**What you need:**

- *a toy play set of the park, the seaside, or playground*
- *small world people*

**Ready for more?**

Look at your garden together and ask your child to tell you the safe places to play. Emphasise *safety* not *danger*.

**WHAT TO DO:**

*This game gives you an opportunity to talk with your child about personal safety.*

1. Set out the play set and small world people.

2. Give plenty of time for your child to play freely with the set before asking some questions.

3. Start to ask some neutral questions about safety – 'Is this boy safe when I put him here?' 'Is this a safe place to play?' and talk about the safe and risky places to play – on the road, near water, very high up, out of sight of adults.

4. Don't go on too long or the questions can worry or put pressure on your child.

**Another idea:** Every time you go out as a family, remind children of the safe places to play.

What is your child learning?

*Role-play with small world toys is a very good way of learning about safety and safe places to play. When children are out in the world, this play will stand them in good stead and enable them to think for themselves.*

### HELPFUL HINTS

Some children find it difficult to tell the difference between safe and dangerous. Keep talking about safe places and behaviours in simple language.

Teach your child the Green Cross Code and give them some responsibility for their own safety, without making them anxious.